Do It Yourself Credit Repair Course

AND

Do It Yourself Building Personal Credit Course

Dr. Angie Locus-Kelly

Each One Reach One Radical Generation, Inc.
FinancialFreedomVIP.com angie@financialfreedomvip.com

Table of Contents

Financial Freedom
by Faith LLC

Website: financialfreedomvip.com Email:
angie@financialfreedomvip.com

CREDIT REPAIR GUIDE
PART 1

STEP 1
HOW TO PULL YOUR CREDIT REPORTS (DETAILED)

Before you can repair your credit, you MUST know what is being reported about you. This step explains exactly how to download all three credit reports: Equifax, Experian, and TransUnion.

A- The BEST and FREE Option

AnnualCreditReport.com is the ONLY federally authorized website to give you all three credit reports for free.

Steps:

1. Go to AnnualCreditReport.com
2. Click "Request Your Free Credit Reports"
3. Enter your personal information
4. Select ALL THREE bureaus
5. Answer security questions
6. Download and save each report as a PDF

B- If the Verification Fails

If the website cannot verify your identity, it will give you instructions to mail in your request instead.

C- Optional Paid Report Sites (Not required)

These sites give cleaner, easier-to-read reports:

- SmartCredit.com – includes score tracking
- IdentityIQ.com – daily monitoring and 3-bureau updates
- MyFICO.com – shows lender-used FICO scores

STEP 2
WHAT TO LOOK FOR ON YOUR CREDIT REPORTS

Your entire credit repair process depends on what you identify in this step. You MUST review your reports line by line for errors, inconsistencies, and unverifiable information.

A- Review ALL Personal Information

Look for:

- Wrong spelling of your name
- Old names or aliases you never used
- Wrong addresses or places you've never lived
- Employers you never worked for
- Incorrect birthdate
- Incorrect SSN digits

Why this matters: Incorrect personal information can connect you to someone else's credit history.

B- Look for Duplicate Accounts

Duplicate accounts hurt your credit because they:

- Double your debt
- Double your negative history
- Make your score look worse

C- Check ALL Dates

Check for wrong:

- Date opened
- Date of last payment

- Date of last activity

- Date reported

Why this matters: Wrong dates can make negative accounts stay longer on your report.

D- Wrong Balances or Status

Examples of inaccurate reporting:

- Balance is too high

- Account marked "late" when paid on time

- Account marked "open" when closed

- Collection shows a balance even if paid

E- Accounts That Should NOT Be There

Includes:

- Fraud

- Mixed files

- Someone else's accounts showing on your report

F- Negative Accounts Over 7 Years Old

Most negative accounts MUST be removed after 7 years from the Date of First Delinquency (DOFD).

G- Compare All Three Bureau Reports

Experian, Equifax, and TransUnion will NOT match. You dispute the differences.

STEP 3
WHAT TO DISPUTE & WHAT NOT TO DISPUTE

A- WHAT TO DISPUTE

1. Incorrect Personal Information

Wrong names, addresses, phone numbers, employers, DOB, or SSN.

2. Accounts You Do NOT Recognize

This includes identity theft, fraudulent accounts, and mixed files.

3. Duplicate Accounts

Accounts reported more than once with different account numbers.

4. Wrong Dates or Wrong Balances

Any inaccurate detail allows the entire account to be disputed.

5. Old Negative Accounts (Over 7 Years)

These MUST be removed by law.

6. Unverifiable Collection Accounts

If a collector cannot prove ownership, the account can be removed.

7. Unauthorized Hard Inquiries

You can dispute inquiries you did NOT approve.

B- WHAT NOT TO DISPUTE

1. Positive Accounts

Do NOT dispute any accounts helping your score.

2. **Active, Current Accounts in Good Standing**

    Never dispute current loans or credit cards you are paying on time.

3. **Accurate Accounts You Legitimately Owe**

    If everything is accurate, you focus on payoff—not disputes.

4. **Accurate Hard Inquiries**

    Only dispute unauthorized ones, never legitimate ones.

TIP: Only dispute ACCOUNT ITEMS that are inaccurate, incomplete, or cannot be verified. Do NOT dispute everything blindly—this can trigger frivolous flags.

CREDIT REPAIR GUIDE
PART 2
(Steps 4–6)

STEP 4
UNDERSTANDING THE CREDIT LAWS (DETAILED)

These are the federal laws that protect consumers during the credit repair process. You do NOT need to be an attorney to use them — just understand your rights clearly.

A- FCRA — Fair Credit Reporting Act

Your rights under the FCRA:

- You can dispute any inaccurate, incomplete, or unverifiable item.
- Credit bureaus MUST investigate within 30 days.
- If the furnisher cannot verify the account with documentation, it MUST be deleted.
- You must receive written results of the investigation.
- You can request the "method of verification."
- You have the right to dispute directly with the creditor or collection agency.

B- FDCPA — Fair Debt Collection Practices Act

This law protects you from abusive debt collectors. Your rights under the FDCPA:

- You can request written validation of any collection.
- Collectors must stop collection until they validate the debt.
- They cannot harass, threaten, or mislead you.
- They must prove they have the right to collect the debt.
- They cannot report unverifiable debt to the bureaus.

C- FCBA — Fair Credit Billing Act

Protects consumers from credit card billing errors. You may dispute:

- Unauthorized charges
- Charges for goods never received
- Charges for services not performed as agreed

D- ECOA — Equal Credit Opportunity Act

Prevents discrimination in lending decisions. Protects against denial of credit based on race, religion, sex, national origin, age, or public assistance income.

STEP 5
ROUND 1 DISPUTES (FULL STEP-BY-STEP)

Round 1 is the "accuracy cleanup" round. Your goal is simple: remove easy errors, incorrect data, and obvious mistakes.

A- What You Need Before Starting Round 1

- Your three credit reports
- A highlighter or pen
- A copy of your Round 1 dispute letter
- Optional supporting documents

B- Choose Which Items to Dispute First

Start with only 2–5 items per bureau. Examples:

- Wrong balance
- Wrong open date
- Duplicate accounts
- Old collections older than 7 years
- Wrong personal information

C- Fill Out Your Round 1 Dispute Letter

Your letter must include:

- Your name and address
- Bureau mailing address
- List of items you dispute
- Explanation of what is inaccurate
- Request for correction or deletion

D- How to Mail Your Disputes

Always use:

Certified Mail with Return Receipt

This gives you proof that the bureau received your disputes.

E- What Happens After Mailing Round 1

The credit bureaus must:

- Begin an investigation within 30 days
- Contact the furnisher of the information
- Review documentation
- Delete or correct inaccuracies
- Send written investigation results

STEP 6
UNDERSTANDING INVESTIGATION RESULTS (DETAILED)

After Round 1, you will receive a results letter from each bureau. There are three possible

outcomes.

1- "DELETED"

This is the BEST outcome. The account is completely removed. No further action needed.

2- "UPDATED"

The item remains but has been changed. If the update is STILL wrong, you move to Round 2 for reinvestigation.

3- "VERIFIED"

This does NOT mean the account is valid — it means the furnisher CLAIMED it is valid. These items ALWAYS move to Round 2.

Tracking Your Disputes

Use a dispute tracking sheet to record:

- Date you mailed your dispute
- Items disputed
- Bureau response
- Next steps needed

If a bureau fails to respond within 30 days

This is an FCRA violation. You can demand deletion OR escalate with a CFPB complaint in Step 10.

CREDIT REPAIR GUIDE
PART 3
(Steps 7–10)

STEP 7
ROUND 2 DISPUTES (REINVESTIGATION – FULL DETAIL)

Round 2 is the reinvestigation stage. It is used when the credit bureaus return an item as "verified" or "updated," but the information is STILL inaccurate, incomplete, or unverifiable.

A- What Round 2 Is Designed To Do

Round 2 forces the bureaus and furnishers to:

- Provide REAL documentation
- Provide the method of verification
- Prove the accuracy of the account
- Show who verified the information

Most furnishers cannot produce proper documentation, which results in deletions.

B- When To Use Round 2

Use this round if:

- An item was "verified" but still wrong
- The bureau updated information incorrectly
- The bureau did not fully address the dispute
- The furnisher did not provide proper verification

C- What to Include in a Round 2 Letter

A Round 2 letter demands deeper investigation and proof:

- Request "method of verification"
- Request documentation used to verify the account

- Explain why the previous investigation was insufficient

- Request deletion if they cannot verify

D- How to Send Your Round 2 Letter

Always send Round 2 by:

Certified Mail with Return Receipt

Never dispute online during Round 2.

E- What Happens Next

The bureau has 30 days to complete a reinvestigation. If the furnisher cannot provide documents, the item must be deleted.

STEP 8
DEBT VALIDATION (FULL FDCPA BREAKDOWN)

Debt validation is the process of forcing a collection agency to PROVE that the debt is valid, accurate, and legally collectible. This step uses the FDCPA (Fair Debt Collection Practices Act).

A- When to Use Debt Validation

Use this step ONLY when the account is in collections. Do NOT send validation letters to original creditors.

B- What You Can Demand in a Debt Validation Letter

You may request:

- Proof they own the debt
- Proof they have the right to collect the debt
- Full account history
- Original signed contract
- Statement of how the amount was calculated
- Chain of custody (proof of legal transfer)
- Collector's license (if required by your state)

C- Collector Requirements

After receiving your validation request, collectors MUST:

- Stop collection immediately
- Stop reporting the account until validated
- Provide full written validation before continuing collection

D- What Their Response May Look Like

Possible outcomes:

1. They validate properly — rare

2. They send insufficient documentation — challenge again

3. They do not respond — BEST outcome; account is unvalidated and cannot remain

E- How to Use Non-Response to Your Advantage

If they don't validate, you may dispute again with the bureaus for deletion.

STEP 9
NEGOTIATING OR SETTLING VALID DEBT (FULL DETAIL)

Negotiation is ONLY used when the debt is fully validated and accurate. NEVER negotiate debt that is incorrect or unverified.

A- When Negotiation Is Necessary

Negotiate if:

- You need fast resolution
- You are trying to qualify for a mortgage or loan
- The collector validated the debt properly

B- Types of Negotiations

1. **Pay-for-Delete (BEST OPTION)**

   You pay an agreed amount; they delete the account from all three bureaus.

2. **Settlement for Less**

   You pay a reduced amount (30–60%). The account updates as "settled for less" but may remain.

3. **Full Payment**

   Used only if needed for mortgage approval or legal reasons.

C- Rules for Safe Negotiation

- Never give collectors access to your bank account
- Only use money orders or cashier's checks
- Get ALL agreements in writing BEFORE paying

STEP 10
CFPB COMPLAINTS (FOR NON-COMPLIANCE)

The CFPB (Consumer Financial Protection Bureau) is a federal agency that enforces credit laws. Use this step when bureaus or collectors break the law.

A- When to File a CFPB Complaint

File a complaint if:

- Bureau does not respond in 30 days
- Bureau falsely "verifies" an item
- Collector fails to validate debt
- Incorrect information continues to report

B- How to File a Complaint

1. Go to consumerfinance.gov/complaint
2. Select the category (credit reporting or debt collection)
3. Describe your issue (simple, factual detail)
4. Upload supporting documents
5. Submit the complaint

C- What Happens After You File

- Agency must respond within 15 days
- Many accounts get corrected or deleted
- CFPB forces compliance with federal law

D- If the Issue Is Not Resolved

You may escalate to:

- State Attorney General
- FTC
- Intent-to-Sue letter

HOW I BUILT
MY PERSONAL CREDIT

After Bankruptcy and Other Negative Accounts Were Cleared

Financial Freedom by Faith FinancialFreedomVIP.com
angie@financialfreedomvip.com

INTRODUCTION
WHY I AM SHARING THIS

I am writing this because I lived it. I filed bankruptcy and watched my credit completely fall apart. I dealt with denials, small limits, and the emotional weight of having to start over as an adult. Once my bankruptcy was discharged and negative accounts were cleared, I learned that rebuilding credit is where most people make mistakes, not because they are irresponsible, but because they rush the process or move emotionally instead of strategically.

This guide is not theory. It is not something I read online or watched on YouTube. This is the exact process I followed, including the things I almost did that would have set me back months if I had not stopped myself.

STEP 1 - CONFIRM MY CREDIT WAS ACTUALLY CLEAN

Before applying for any new credit, I pulled all three credit reports from Experian, Equifax, and TransUnion. I did not just look at the score. I reviewed each account line by line. I verified that bankruptcy accounts showed zero balances, that included accounts were marked correctly, and that no old collection accounts were still reporting incorrectly.

I also checked personal identifying information such as name and address to make sure outdated variations were not causing reporting issues. I did nothing else until everything was accurate because applying with incorrect reporting leads to unnecessary denials.

STEP 2 - I STOPPED APPLYING FOR CREDIT

Once my reports were clean, offers started appearing. Pre approved mailers, emails, and pop ups all made it seem like I was ready to apply everywhere. This is where many people mess up. Offers are marketing tools, not trust indicators. I stopped applying completely and let my reports stabilize.

By pausing, I protected myself from stacking inquiries and from creating a credit profile that looked desperate or unstable to lenders.

STEP 3 - I OPENED ONE REBUILDING ACCOUNT

When I finally applied, I opened one rebuilding account. I did not open multiple cards just because I could. I focused on managing one account perfectly because one well managed account does more for your credit than several poorly managed ones.

The goal during rebuilding is not variety. The goal is consistency.

STEP 4 - I MANAGED CREDIT USAGE CAREFULLY

I treated my credit limit as if it were lower than it actually was. I kept my utilization under thirty percent and most months aimed closer to ten or twenty percent. Small limits are not punishment. They are testing grounds.

What matters is not just how much you owe but what reports. Balances report when the statement closes, not when the bill is due.

STEP 5 - I PAID BEFORE THE STATEMENT DATE

Paying on time is good. Paying before the statement closes is better. I paid balances early so the bureaus always saw low utilization. This single habit made one of the biggest differences in my rebuild.

Many people pay on the due date and wonder why their scores do not improve. What reports matters more than what is due.

STEP 6 - I ADDED CREDIT SLOWLY

Instead of opening new accounts, I requested credit limit increases and confirmed whether those requests would require hard inquiries. I added additional credit only when my existing account showed consistent positive behavior.

One strong account always beats several weak ones.

STEP 7 - I STAYED CONSISTENT

Rebuilding credit is not about one big move. It is about repeating the same responsible behavior month after month. Consistency builds trust over time.

On time payments, low balances, and no unnecessary activity were the foundation of my rebuild.

IMPORTANT LESSON ABOUT BANKRUPTCY

Chapter seven bankruptcy can remain on a credit report for up to ten years and chapter thirteen for up to seven. However rebuilding can begin much sooner. Many people start receiving offers within nine to eighteen months after discharge.

Small starting limits are normal. The goal is not to be offended by them but to manage them properly.

THE MISTAKES I ALMOST MADE

I almost applied too fast. I almost used too much of a small limit. I almost paid on the due date instead of before the statement closed. Each of these mistakes could have delayed my progress for months.

Avoiding these mistakes saved time, stress, and unnecessary setbacks.

THE DO AND DO NOT LIST

Do stay patient. Do pay early. Do keep balances low. Do stay consistent. Do not rush. Do not apply emotionally. Do not chase approvals.

RECOMMENDED STARTER CARDS

Capital One Platinum and Discover secured or unsecured cards are examples of rebuilding tools. I did not apply for all of them. I chose one based on timing and profile readiness.

WHAT TO SAY WHEN YOU CALL

I kept calls short and professional. I asked clear questions and avoided emotional explanations. Credit conversations are data conversations.

THIRTY SIXTY NINETY DAY PLAN

First thirty days focus on accuracy. Days thirty one through sixty focus on consistency. Days sixty one through ninety focus on reviewing progress and requesting increases if appropriate.

FINAL WORD

You are not starting over in life. You are starting over on paper. That paper can be rewritten carefully and intentionally if you respect the process.

DISCLAIMER

This guide is for educational purposes only and reflects personal experience. Results vary by individual and lender.

This book is for individuals ready to take control of their credit—step by step.

Inside this guide, Dr. Angie Locus-Kelly shares real-life experience rebuilding credit after financial hardship. This is not theory. This is a clear, structured, do-it-yourself approach designed to help you understand, repair, and rebuild personal credit responsibly and legally.

Created as an educational resource through Each One Reach One Radical Generation, Inc., this book is suitable for community programs, reentry support, and personal financial restoration.

FinancialFreedomVIP.com
angie@financialfreedomvip.com

Financial Freedom
By Faith LLC

Dr. Angie Kelly

Credit Repair Sample Letters

DIY Credit Repair Package

Wrong Name Dispute

Name: ____

Address: ____

City/State/ZIP: ____

Date: ____

Credit Bureau: ____

Subject: ____

Wrong Name Dispute (FCRA §607(b), §611) To Whom It May Concern,

I am writing to dispute an incorrect name that is appearing on my credit report. The name listed below does not belong to me:

Incorrect Name Appearing: ____________________________________

My correct legal name is: _____________________________________

Under FCRA §607(b), all information on a credit report must be accurate.

Under FCRA §611, I am requesting a reinvestigation and correction of this error.

Explanation (optional): _______________________________________

Sincerely,____

Wrong Address Dispute

Name: ____

Address: ____

City/State/ZIP: ____

Date: ____

Credit Bureau: ____

Subject: ____

Wrong Address Dispute (FCRA §607(b), §611) To Whom It May Concern,

I am writing to dispute an incorrect address that appears on my credit report. This address does not belong to me:

Incorrect Address: ____

My correct address is: _______________________________________

Under FCRA §607(b), credit bureaus must ensure maximum accuracy. Under FCRA §611, I request a reinvestigation and correction.

Explanation (optional): ______________________________________

Sincerely,____

Mixed File Dispute

Name: ____

Address: ____
City/State/ZIP: _____________________________________

Date: ____

Credit Bureau: ______________________________________

Subject: ____

Mixed File Dispute (FCRA §607(b), §611) To Whom It May Concern,

I am writing to dispute accounts and information appearing on my credit file that do not belong to me. My file appears to be mixed with another individual.

Incorrect or Not-Mine Information:

Under FCRA §607(b), you must maintain accurate file separation. Under FCRA §611, I request immediate correction and reinvestigation.

Explanation (optional): ____

Sincerely,____

Account Not Mine Dispute

Name: ____

Address: ____

City/State/ZIP: ____

Date: ____

Credit Bureau: ____

Subject: ____

Account Not Mine Dispute (FCRA §611, §605B) To Whom It May Concern,

I am disputing the following account that does NOT belong to me: Account Name/Number: ____

Under FCRA §605B, fraudulent or not-mine accounts must be blocked. Under FCRA §611, I request a full reinvestigation.

Explanation (optional): ____

Sincerely, ____

Incorrect Account Information Dispute

Name: ____

Address: ____

City/State/ZIP: ____

Date: ____

Credit Bureau: ____

Subject: ____

Incorrect Account Information (FCRA §607(b), §611) To Whom It May Concern,

I am writing to dispute inaccurate information reported on the account below: ____

Account Name/Number: ______________________________________

Inaccurate Details (balance/date/status): ____________________

Under FCRA §607(b), information must be complete and accurate. Under FCRA §611, I request correction and an updated credit report.

Explanation (optional): _____________________________________

Sincerely, ____

Bankruptcy Reporting Error Dispute

Name: ____

Address: ____

City/State/ZIP: ____

Date: ____

Credit Bureau: ____

Subject: ____

Bankruptcy Reporting Error (FCRA §607(b), §611) To Whom It May Concern,

I am disputing inaccurate bankruptcy reporting on my credit file. Incorrect Bankruptcy Information: ________________________________

Under FCRA §607(b), all reported information must be accurate. Under FCRA §611, I request a full reinvestigation and correction.

Explanation (optional): _____________________________________

Sincerely, ____

Re-Aging Dispute

Name: ____

Address: ____

City/State/ZIP: ______________________________________

Date: ____

Credit Bureau: _______________________________________

Subject: ____

Illegal Re-Aging Dispute (FCRA §607(b), §611) To Whom It May Concern,

I am disputing the re-aging of the following account: Account Name/Number: _________________________________

The dates reported do not match the original delinquency date. Under FCRA §607(b), re-aging is prohibited.

Under FCRA §611, I request correction and reinvestigation.

Sincerely, ____

Reinsertion Dispute

Name: ____

Address: ____

City/State/ZIP: ____

Date: ____

Credit Bureau: ____

Subject: ____

Reinsertion of Deleted Item (FCRA §611(a)(5)) To Whom It May Concern,

A previously deleted item has reappeared on my credit report. Account/Item: ____

Under FCRA §611(a)(5), reinsertion requires certification of accuracy. I request removal unless proper certification is provided.

Sincerely, ____

Student Loan Reporting Dispute

Name: ____

Address: ____

City/State/ZIP: ____

Date: ____

Credit Bureau: ____

Subject: ____

Student Loan Reporting Dispute (FCRA §607(b), §611) To Whom It May Concern,

I am disputing incorrect student loan reporting on the following account: Loan Servicer/Number: ____

Incorrect Details: ____

Under FCRA §607(b), information must be accurate.

Under FCRA §611, I request correction and reinvestigation.

Sincerely, ____

Medical/HIPAA Reporting Dispute

Name: ____

Address: ____

City/State/ZIP: ____

Date: ____

Credit Bureau: ____

Subject: ____

Medical Account Reporting Dispute (FCRA §607(b), HIPAA Privacy Rule)
To Whom It May Concern,

I am disputing the reporting of a medical-related account on my credit
file. Medical Provider/Account: _______________________________________

Under HIPAA and FCRA §607(b), private medical details cannot be
reported. I request correction or removal.

Sincerely, ____

Late Payment Dispute

Name: ____

Address: ____

City/State/ZIP: ____

Date: ____

Credit Bureau: ____

Subject: ____

Late Payment Dispute (FCRA §607(b), §611) To Whom It May Concern,

I am disputing the reporting of a late payment on the account below:
Account Name/Number: ____

This late payment is inaccurate or does not reflect my actual payment history. Under FCRA §607(b), information reported must be accurate.

Under FCRA §611, I request a reinvestigation and correction.

Explanation (optional): ______________________________________

Sincerely, ____

Charge-Off Dispute

Name: ____

Address: ____

City/State/ZIP: ____

Date: ____

Credit Bureau: ____

Subject: ____

Charge-Off Reporting Dispute (FCRA §607(b), §611) To Whom It May Concern,

I am disputing inaccurate charge-off reporting on the following account: Account Name/Number: _____________________________________

Incorrect Details (balance/date/status):

Under FCRA §607(b), credit information must be accurate. Under FCRA §611, I request a reinvestigation and correction.

Sincerely, ____

609 Request Letter

Name: ____

Address: ____

City/State/ZIP: ____

Date: ____

Credit Bureau: ____

Subject: ____

FCRA 609 Request for Documentation (FCRA §609) To Whom It May Concern,

I am requesting all source documents used to verify and report the account below: ____

Account Name/Number: ____

Under FCRA §609, I have the right to request all records used to validate reporting. Please provide copies of:

- Signed contract or application

- Account verification documents

- All information used to verify ownership Sincerely,

611 Reinvestigation Letter

Name: ____

Address: ____

City/State/ZIP: ____

Date: ____

Credit Bureau: ____

Subject: ____

FCRA 611 Reinvestigation Request (FCRA §611) To Whom It May Concern,

I am requesting a reinvestigation of the following item due to inaccurate reporting: ____

Item or Account: ____

Under FCRA §611, you must investigate and provide results within 30 days. Explanation (optional): ____________________________________

Sincerely, ____

623 Direct Dispute Letter

Name: ____

Address: ____

City/State/ZIP: _______________________________________

Date: ____

Credit Bureau: _______________________________________

Subject: ____

Direct Dispute to Furnisher (FCRA §623) To Whom It May Concern,

I am disputing inaccurate information your company is furnishing to the credit bureaus regarding the following account:

Account Name/Number: ________________________________

Inaccurate Details: ____________________________________

Under FCRA §623, furnishers must investigate disputed information and correct any inaccuracies.

Sincerely,____

Debt Validation Request

Name: ____

Address: ____

City/State/ZIP: ______________________________________

Date: ____

Creditor/Collector: __________________________________

Subject: ____

Debt Validation Request (FDCPA §1692g) To Whom It May Concern,

I am requesting full validation of the debt listed below: Collection Agency/Account: _____________________________________

Under FDCPA §1692g, you must provide proof of:

- Original creditor

- Documentation of the debt

- Verification of accuracy

Sincerely,____

Verification of Accuracy

Name: ____

Address: ____

City/State/ZIP: ____

Date: ____

Creditor/Collector: ____

Subject: ____

Verification of Accuracy (FDCPA §1692e, FCRA §611) To Whom It May Concern,

I am disputing the accuracy of the following collection account: __________

Account: ____

Under FDCPA §1692e and FCRA §611, furnishers must verify accuracy.

Sincerely,____

Proof of Ownership / Chain of Custody

Name: ____

Address: ____

City/State/ZIP: ____________________________________

Date: ____

Creditor/Collector: ________________________________

Subject: ____

Proof of Ownership Request (FDCPA §1692g) To Whom It May Concern,

I am requesting proof of ownership and chain of custody for: ____________

Account: ____

Provide documentation showing legal right to collect this debt.

Sincerely, ____

Cease & Desist Letter

Name: ____

Address: ____

City/State/ZIP: ____

Date: ____

Creditor/Collector: ____

Subject: ____

 Cease and Desist (FDCPA §1692c(c)) To Whom It May Concern,

I am requesting that you cease all communication regarding the account listed below.

Account: ____

Under FDCPA §1692c(c), communication must stop except for legal notices.

Sincerely, ____

Notice of Violations

Name: ____

Address: ____

City/State/ZIP: ____

Date: ____

Creditor/Collector: ____

Subject: ____

Notice of Violations (FDCPA §1692d, §1692e) To Whom It May Concern,

Your agency has violated the FDCPA regarding the following account: ____

Account:____

Under FDCPA §1692d and §1692e, harassment and misleading information are prohibited.

Sincerely,____

Pay-for-Delete Letter

Name: ____

Address: ____

City/State/ZIP: ____

Date: ____

Creditor/Collector: ____

Subject: ____

Pay-for-Delete Agreement Request (FCRA §607(b)) To Whom It May Concern,

I am requesting a pay-for-delete arrangement for the following account:
____

Creditor/Account: ____

I am willing to pay an agreed-upon amount in exchange for complete removal of this account from all credit bureau reports.

Please provide written confirmation before payment.

Sincerely, ____

Goodwill Removal Letter

Name: ____

Address: ____

City/State/ZIP: _______________________________________

Date: ____

Creditor/Collector: ____________________________________

Subject: ____

Goodwill Adjustment Request To Whom It May Concern,

I am requesting a goodwill removal of the following negative entry: ______

Creditor/Account: _____________________________________

I have maintained a positive relationship and ask for a courtesy adjustment.

Sincerely, ____

Settlement-in-Full Letter

Name: ____

Address: ____

City/State/ZIP: ____

Date: ____

Creditor/Collector: ____

Subject: ____

Settlement in Full Agreement To Whom It May Concern,

I am offering a settlement in full for the following account: ____________

Creditor/Account: ____

Please provide written confirmation that payment will satisfy the debt entirely.

Sincerely, ____

Settlement with Conditions

Name: ____

Address: ____

City/State/ZIP: ____

Date: ____

Creditor/Collector: ____

Subject: ____

Conditional Settlement Agreement To Whom It May Concern,

I am offering conditional settlement for the following account: ___________

Creditor/Account: ____

Conditions:

- Account reported as paid or settled

- No further collection activity

Provide written confirmation before payment. Sincerely,

Fraud / Identity Theft Affidavit Letter

Name: ____

Address: ____

City/State/ZIP: ____

Date: ____

Creditor/Collector: ____

Subject: Fraud/Identity Theft Dispute (FCRA §605B) To Whom It May Concern,

I am disputing the following as fraud/identity theft: ______________________

Creditor/Account: ____

Under FCRA §605B, block all fraudulent accounts immediately.

Sincerely,____